MznLnx

Missing Links Exam Preps

Exam Prep for

Mathematics Beyond the Numbers

Gilbert & Hatcher, 1st Edition

The MznLnx Exam Prep is your link from the texbook and lecture to your exams.
The MznLnx Exam Preps are unauthorized and comprehensive reviews of your textbooks.

All material provided by MznLnx and Rico Publications (c) 2010
Textbook publishers and textbook authors do not particpate in or contribute to these reviews.

MznLnx

Rico
Publications

Exam Prep for Mathematics Beyond the Numbers
1st Edition
Gilbert & Hatcher

Publisher: Raymond Houge
Assistant Editor: Michael Rouger
Text and Cover Designer: Lisa Buckner
Marketing Manager: Sara Swagger
Project Manager, Editorial Production: Jerry Emerson
Art Director: Vernon Lowerui

Product Manager: Dave Mason
Editorial Assitant: Rachel Guzmanji
Pedagogy: Debra Long
Cover Image: Jim Reed/Getty Images
Text and Cover Printer: City Printing, Inc.
Compositor: Media Mix, Inc.

(c) 2010 Rico Publications
ALL RIGHTS RESERVED. No part of this work covered by the copyright may be reproduced or used in any form or by an means--graphic, electronic, or mechanical, including photocopying, recording, taping, Web distribution, information storage, and retrieval systems, or in any other manner--without the written permission of the publisher.

Printed in the United States
ISBN:

For more information about our products, contact us at:
Dave.Mason@RicoPublications.com

For permission to use material from this text or product, submit a request online to:
Dave.Mason@RicoPublications.com

Contents

CHAPTER 1
Voting Methods — 1

CHAPTER 2
Apportionment: Sharing What Cannot Be Divided Arbitrarily — 5

CHAPTER 3
The Mathematics of Money — 8

CHAPTER 4
Probability — 14

CHAPTER 5
Statistics — 21

CHAPTER 6
Paths and Networks — 33

CHAPTER 7
Tilings and Polyhedra — 40

CHAPTER 8
Number Theory — 46

CHAPTER 9
Game Theory with an Introduction to Linear Programming — 60

ANSWER KEY — 67

TO THE STUDENT

COMPREHENSIVE

The *MznLnx* Exam Prep series is designed to help you pass your exams. Editors at MznLnx review your textbooks and then prepare these practice exams to help you master the textbook material. Unlike study guides, workbooks, and practice tests provided by the texbook publisher and textbook authors, *MznLnx* gives you **all** of the material in each chapter in exam form, not just samples, so you can be sure to nail your exam.

MECHANICAL

The MznLnx Exam Prep series creates exams that will help you learn the subject matter as well as test you on your understanding. Each question is designed to help you master the concept. Just working through the exams, you gain an understanding of the subject--its a simple mechanical process that produces success.

INTEGRATED STUDY GUIDE AND REVIEW

MznLnx is not just a set of exams designed to test you, its also a comprehensive review of the subject content. Each exam question is also a review of the concept, making sure that you will get the answer correct without having to go to other sources of material. You learn as you go! Its the easiest way to pass an exam.

HUMOR

Studying can be tedious and dry. MznLnx's instructional design includes moderate humor within the exam questions on occassion, to break the tedium and revitalize the brain

Chapter 1. Voting Methods

1. A _____ is often defined as a geometric object with flat faces and straight edges.

This definition of a _____ is not very precise, and to a modern mathematician is quite unsatisfactory. Grünbaum observed that:

The Original Sin in the theory of polyhedra goes back to Euclid, and through Kepler, Poinsot, Cauchy and many others ...

   a. 2-3 heap
   b. Polyhedron
   c. 1-center problem
   d. 120-cell

2. An _____ is a decision-making process by which a population chooses an individual to hold formal office. This is the usual mechanism by which modern democracy fills offices in the legislature, sometimes in the executive and judiciary, and for regional and local government. This process is also used in many other private and business organizations, from clubs to voluntary associations and corporations.
   a. A posteriori
   b. A Mathematical Theory of Communication
   c. Election
   d. A chemical equation

3. A _____ is a relationship between a set of items such that, for any two items, the first is either 'ranked higher than', 'ranked lower than' or 'ranked equal to' the second. In mathematics, this is known as a weak order or total preorder of objects. It is not necessarily a total order of objects because two different objects can have the same _____.
   a. Ranking
   b. Kernel smoother
   c. 1-center problem
   d. Non-parametric statistic

4. In mathematics, a _____ is a way of expressing a number as a fraction of 100. It is often denoted using the percent sign, '%'. For example, 45% is equal to 45 / 100, or 0.45.
   a. Lowest common denominator
   b. Least common multiple
   c. Subtrahend
   d. Percentage

Chapter 1. Voting Methods

5. The _____ is a single-winner election method in which voters rank candidates in order of preference. The _____ determines the winner of an election by giving each candidate a certain number of points corresponding to the position in which he or she is ranked by each voter. Once all votes have been counted the candidate with the most points is the winner.
    a. 120-cell
    b. 1-center problem
    c. 2-3 heap
    d. Borda count

6. The Condorcet candidate or _____ of an election is the candidate who, when compared with every other candidate, is preferred by more voters. Informally, the _____ is the person who would win a two-candidate election against each of the other candidates. A _____ will not always exist in a given set of votes, which is known as Condorcet's voting paradox.
    a. 1-center problem
    b. Psephology
    c. 120-cell
    d. Condorcet winner

7. _____ is the word given to a number of similar team sports, all of which involve (to varying degrees) kicking a ball with the foot in an attempt to score a goal. The most popular of these sports worldwide is association _____, more commonly known as just '_____' or 'soccer'. The English language word '_____' is also applied to 'gridiron _____' (a name associated with the North American sports, especially American _____ and Canadian _____), Australian _____, Gaelic _____, rugby _____ (rugby league and rugby union), and related games.
    a. Football
    b. 2-3 heap
    c. 1-center problem
    d. 120-cell

8. In commutative algebra, the term _____ refers to several related functors on topological rings and modules. _____ is similar to localization, and together they are among the most basic tools in analysing commutative rings. Complete commutative rings have simpler structure than the general ones, in large part, due to Hensel's lemma.
    a. Decimal system
    b. Battle of the Sexes
    c. Colossus
    d. Completion

Chapter 1. Voting Methods

9. _____ is derived from the Greek word ανωνυμῖα, meaning 'without a name' or 'namelessness'. In colloquial use, the term typically refers to a person, and often means that the personal identity, or personally identifiable information of that person is not known.

More strictly, and in reference to an arbitrary element, within a well-defined set, '_____' of that element refers to the property of that element of not being identifiable within this set.

   a. A chemical equation
   b. A Mathematical Theory of Communication
   c. A posteriori
   d. Anonymity

10. _____ is the self-government of a nation, country or some portion thereof, generally exercising sovereignty.

The term _____ is used in contrast to subjugation, which refers to a region as a 'territory' --subject to the political and military control of an external government. The word is sometimes used in a weaker sense to contrast with hegemony, the indirect control of one nation by another, more powerful nation.

   a. A posteriori
   b. Independence
   c. A chemical equation
   d. A Mathematical Theory of Communication

11. _____ is an important concept in economics with broad applications in game theory, engineering and the social sciences. The term is named after Vilfredo Pareto, an Italian economist who used the concept in his studies of economic efficiency and income distribution.

Given a set of alternative allocations of, say, goods or income for a set of individuals, a change from one allocation to another that can make at least one individual better off without making any other individual worse off is called a Pareto improvement.

   a. Pareto efficiency
   b. Quasi-perfect equilibrium
   c. Multiunit auction
   d. Pursuit-evasion

12. In mathematics, a _____ is a statement that can be proved on the basis of explicitly stated or previously agreed assumptions.

a. Theorem
   b. Disjunction introduction
   c. Boolean function
   d. Logical value

13. In mathematics, especially in the area of abstract algebra known as ring theory, a _____ is a ring with 0 ≠ 1 such that ab = 0 implies that either a = 0 or b = 0. That is, it is a nontrivial ring without left or right zero divisors. A commutative _____ is called an integral _____.
   a. Modular representation theory
   b. Left primitive ring
   c. Domain
   d. Simple ring

Chapter 2. Apportionment: Sharing What Cannot Be Divided Arbitrarily

1. In mathematics, a _____ of an integer n is an integer which evenly divides n without leaving a remainder.

For example, 7 is a _____ of 42 because 42/7 = 6. We also say 42 is divisible by 7 or 42 is a multiple of 7 or 7 divides 42 or 7 is a factor of 42 and we usually write 7 | 42.

   a. 1-center problem
   b. 2-3 heap
   c. 120-cell
   d. Divisor

2. In mathematics, the _____ of a number n is the number that, when added to n, yields zero. The _____ of n is denoted −n. For example, 7 is −7, because 7 + (−7) = 0, and the _____ of −0.3 is 0.3, because −0.3 + 0.3 = 0.
   a. Algebraic structure
   b. Associativity
   c. Additive inverse
   d. Arity

3. The word _____ is the Latin ablative of modulus which itself means 'a small measure.' It was introduced into mathematics in the book Disquisitiones Arithmeticae by Carl Friedrich Gauss in 1801. Ever since, however, '_____' has gained many meanings, some exact and some imprecise.

   - (This usage is from Gauss's book.) Given the integers a, b and n, the expression a ≡ b (mod n) means that a − b is a multiple of n, or equivalently, a and b both leave the same remainder when divided by n. For more details, see modular arithmetic.

   - In computing, given two numbers (either integer or real), a and n, a _____ n is the remainder after numerical division of a by n, under certain constraints. See _____ operation.

   a. Quotition
   b. Per mil
   c. Predictor-corrector method
   d. Modulo

4. An _____ is a decision-making process by which a population chooses an individual to hold formal office. This is the usual mechanism by which modern democracy fills offices in the legislature, sometimes in the executive and judiciary, and for regional and local government. This process is also used in many other private and business organizations, from clubs to voluntary associations and corporations.

6   *Chapter 2. Apportionment: Sharing What Cannot Be Divided Arbitrarily*

    a. Election
    b. A posteriori
    c. A Mathematical Theory of Communication
    d. A chemical equation

5. The _____, in mathematics, is a type of mean or average, which indicates the central tendency or typical value of a set of numbers. It is similar to the arithmetic mean, which is what most people think of with the word 'average,' except that instead of adding the set of numbers and then dividing the sum by the count of numbers in the set, n, the numbers are multiplied and then the nth root of the resulting product is taken.

For instance, the _____ of two numbers, say 2 and 8, is just the square root (i.e., the second root) of their product, 16, which is 4.

    a. Stratified sampling
    b. Skewness
    c. Correlation
    d. Geometric mean

6. In statistics, _____ has two related meanings:

- the arithmetic _____.
- the expected value of a random variable, which is also called the population _____.

It is sometimes stated that the '_____' _____s average. This is incorrect if '_____' is taken in the specific sense of 'arithmetic _____' as there are different types of averages: the _____, median, and mode. For instance, average house prices almost always use the median value for the average.

For a real-valued random variable X, the _____ is the expectation of X.

    a. Statistical population
    b. Probability
    c. Proportional hazards model
    d. Mean

7. In mathematics, two quantities are called _____ if they vary in such a way that one of the quantities is a constant multiple of the other, or equivalently if they have a constant ratio.

a. 120-cell
b. 2-3 heap
c. 1-center problem
d. Proportional

8. In mathematics, an _____, or central tendency of a data set refers to a measure of the 'middle' or 'expected' value of the data set. There are many different descriptive statistics that can be chosen as a measurement of the central tendency of the data items.

An _____ is a single value that is meant to typify a list of values.

a. A Mathematical Theory of Communication
b. A chemical equation
c. A posteriori
d. Average

9. The _____ was the first of the apportionment paradoxes to be discovered. The US House of Representatives is Constitutionally required to allocate seats based on population counts, which are required every 10 years. The size of the House is set by statute.
a. Infinity
b. Alabama paradox
c. Implicit differentiation
d. A Mathematical Theory of Communication

10. In mathematics, a _____ is a statement that can be proved on the basis of explicitly stated or previously agreed assumptions.
a. Disjunction introduction
b. Boolean function
c. Logical value
d. Theorem

Chapter 3. The Mathematics of Money

1. In statistics, a _____ is a graphical display of tabulated frequencies, shown as bars. It shows what proportion of cases fall into each of several categories. A _____ differs from a bar chart in that it is the area of the bar that denotes the value, not the height as in bar charts, a crucial distinction when the categories are not of uniform width.
    a. First-hitting-time models
    b. Probability distribution
    c. Standardized moment
    d. Histogram

2. In vascular plants, the _____ is the organ of a plant body that typically lies below the surface of the soil. This is not always the case, however, since a _____ can also be aerial (that is, growing above the ground) or aerating (that is, growing up above the ground or especially above water.) Furthermore, a stem normally occurring below ground is not exceptional either
    a. 120-cell
    b. 2-3 heap
    c. 1-center problem
    d. Root

3. In mathematics, the _____ of a number to a given base is the power or exponent to which the base must be raised in order to produce the number.

    For example, the _____ of 1000 to the base 10 is 3, because 3 is how many 10s one must multiply to get 1000: thus 10 × 10 × 10 = 1000; the base-2 _____ of 32 is 5 because 5 is how many 2s one must multiply to get 32: thus 2 × 2 × 2 × 2 × 2 = 32. In the language of exponents: 10^3 = 1000, so $\log_{10} 1000 = 3$, and 2^5 = 32, so $\log_2 32 = 5$.

    a. 2-3 heap
    b. 120-cell
    c. 1-center problem
    d. Logarithm

4. The _____ is a mechanical analog computer. The _____ is used primarily for multiplication and division, and also for 'scientific' functions such as roots, logarithms and trigonometry, but does not generally perform addition or subtraction.

    _____s come in a diverse range of styles and generally appear in a linear or circular form with a standardized set of markings essential to performing mathematical computations.

a. 120-cell
b. 1-center problem
c. Slide rule
d. 2-3 heap

5. In abstract algebra, a module S over a ring R is called _____ or irreducible if it is not the zero module 0 and if its only submodules are 0 and S. Understanding the _____ modules over a ring is usually helpful because these modules form the 'building blocks' of all other modules in a certain sense.

Abelian groups are the same as Z-modules.

a. Simple
b. Basis
c. Derivation
d. Harmonic series

6. _____ is a fee, paid on borrowed capital. Assets lent include money, shares, consumer goods through hire purchase, major assets such as aircraft, and even entire factories in finance lease arrangements. The _____ is calculated upon the value of the assets in the same manner as upon money.

a. A Mathematical Theory of Communication
b. Interest sensitivity gap
c. Interest expense
d. Interest

7. In mathematics and in the sciences, a _____ (plural: _____e, formulæ or _____s) is a concise way of expressing information symbolically (as in a mathematical or chemical _____), or a general relationship between quantities. One of many famous _____e is Albert Einstein's E = mc^2 (see special relativity

In mathematics, a _____ is a key to solve an equation with variables. For example, the problem of determining the volume of a sphere is one that requires a significant amount of integral calculus to solve.

a. 2-3 heap
b. 120-cell
c. 1-center problem
d. Formula

Chapter 3. The Mathematics of Money

8. _____ is the concept of adding accumulated interest back to the principal, so that interest is earned on interest from that moment on. The act of declaring interest to be principal is called compounding. A loan, for example, may have its interest compounded every month: in this case, a loan with $100 principal and 1% interest per month would have a balance of $101 at the end of the first month.
   a. Retained interest
   b. Net interest margin
   c. Compound interest
   d. Net interest margin securities

9. In mathematics, a _____ is a number that can be expressed as an integral of an algebraic function over an algebraic domain. Kontsevich and Zagier define a _____ as a complex number whose real and imaginary parts are values of absolutely convergent integrals of rational functions with rational coefficients, over domains in given by polynomial inequalities with rational coefficients.
   a. Boussinesq approximation
   b. Closeness
   c. Disk
   d. Period

10. _____ expresses an annual rate of interest taking into account the effect of compounding, usually for deposit or investment products. It is analogous to the Annual percentage rate, which is used for loans. In some jurisdictions, the use and definition of _____ may be regulated by a government agency, in which case it would generally be capitalized.
    a. A Mathematical Theory of Communication
    b. Annual percentage yield
    c. A posteriori
    d. A chemical equation

11. In mathematics, a _____ is a way of expressing a number as a fraction of 100. It is often denoted using the percent sign, '%'. For example, 45% is equal to 45 / 100, or 0.45.
    a. Least common multiple
    b. Lowest common denominator
    c. Subtrahend
    d. Percentage

12. In mathematics, a _____ is a series with a constant ratio between successive terms. For example, the series

Chapter 3. The Mathematics of Money

$$\frac{1}{2} + \frac{1}{4} + \frac{1}{8} + \frac{1}{16} + \cdots$$

is geometric, because each term is equal to half of the previous term. The sum of this series is 1, as illustrated in the following picture:

_____ are one of the simplest examples of infinite series with finite sums.

a. Riemann series theorem
b. Telescoping series
c. Summation by parts
d. Geometric series

13. In mathematics, a _____ is often represented as the sum of a sequence of terms. That is, a _____ is represented as a list of numbers with addition operations between them, for example this arithmetic sequence:

1 + 2 + 3 + 4 + 5 + ... + 99 + 100

In most cases of interest the terms of the sequence are produced according to a certain rule, such as by a formula, by an algorithm, by a sequence of measurements, or even by a random number generator.

a. Contact
b. Series
c. Blind
d. Concavity

14. The terms _____, nominal APR, and effective APR describe the interest rate for a whole year, rather than just a monthly fee/rate, as applied on a loan, mortgage, credit card, etc. Those terms have formal, legal definitions in some countries or legal jurisdictions, but in general:

- The nominal APR is the simple-interest rate.
- The effective APR is the fee+compound interest rate.

The nominal APR is calculated as: the rate, for a payment period, multiplied by the number of payment periods in a year. However, the exact legal definition of 'effective APR' can vary greatly in each jurisdiction, depending on the type of fees included, such as participation fees, loan origination fees, monthly service charges, or late fees. The effective APR has been called the 'mathematically-true' interest rate for each year. The computation for the effective APR, as the fee+compound interest rate, can also vary depending on whether the up-front fees, such as origination or participation fees, are added to the entire amount, or treated as a short-term loan due in the first payment.

Chapter 3. The Mathematics of Money

a. A posteriori
b. A Mathematical Theory of Communication
c. A chemical equation
d. Annual percentage rate

15. _____ or amortisation is the process of decreasing an amount over a period of time. The word comes from Middle English amortisen to kill, alienate in mortmain, from Anglo-French amorteser, alteration of amortir, from Vulgar Latin admortire to kill, from Latin ad- + mort-, mors death. Particular instances of the term include:

- _____, the allocation of a lump sum amount to different time periods, particularly for loans and other forms of finance, including related interest or other finance charges.
    - _____ schedule, a table detailing each periodic payment on a loan, as generated by an _____ calculator.
    - Negative _____, an _____ schedule where the loan amount actually increases through not paying the full interest
- Amortized analysis, analyzing the execution cost of algorithms over a sequence of operations.
- _____ of capital expenditures of certain assets under accounting rules, particularly intangible assets, in a manner analogous to depreciation.
- _____

_____ is also used in the context of zoning regulations and describes the time in which a property owner has to relocate when the property's use constitutes a preexisting nonconforming use under zoning regulations.

- Depreciation

a. Origin
b. Identity
c. Amortization
d. ISAAC

16. An _____ is a table detailing each periodic payment on a amortizing loan, as generated by an amortization calculator.

While a portion of every payment is applied towards both the interest and the principal balance of the loan, the exact amount applied to principal each time varies. An _____ reveals the specific monetary amount put towards interest, as well as the specific put towards the Principal balance, with each payment.

a. A chemical equation
b. Amortization schedule
c. Accounts receivable
d. A Mathematical Theory of Communication

Chapter 4. Probability

1. In probability theory, an _____ is a set of outcomes to which a probability is assigned. Typically, when the sample space is finite, any subset of the sample space is an _____. However, this approach does not work well in cases where the sample space is infinite, most notably when the outcome is a real number.
    a. Audio compression
    b. Information set
    c. Equaliser
    d. Event

2. In scientific inquiry, an _____ is a method of investigating particular types of research questions or solving particular types of problems. The _____ is a cornerstone in the empirical approach to acquiring deeper knowledge about the world and is used in both natural sciences as well as in social sciences. An _____ is defined, in science, as a method of investigating less known fields, solving practical problems and proving theoretical assumptions.
    a. A posteriori
    b. A chemical equation
    c. A Mathematical Theory of Communication
    d. Experiment

3. In game theory, an _____ is a set of moves or strategies taken by the players, or their payoffs resulting from the actions or strategies taken by all players. The two are complementary in that given knowledge of the set of strategies of all players, the final state of the game is known, as are any relevant payoffs. In a game where chance or a random event is involved, the _____ is not known from only the set of strategies, but is only realized when the random even are realized.
    a. Autonomous system
    b. Equaliser
    c. OutCome
    d. Algebraic

4. _____ is the likelihood or chance that something is the case or will happen. Theoretical _____ is used extensively in areas such as statistics, mathematics, science and philosophy to draw conclusions about the likelihood of potential events and the underlying mechanics of complex systems.

    The word _____ does not have a consistent direct definition.

    a. Probability
    b. Discrete random variable
    c. Standardized moment
    d. Statistical significance

Chapter 4. Probability

5. The word _____ denotes information gained by means of observation, experience as opposed to theoretical. A central concept in science and the scientific method is that all evidence must be _____ that is, dependent on evidence or consequences that are observable by the senses. It is usually differentiated from the philosophic usage of empiricism by the use of the adjective '_____' or the adverb 'empirically.' '_____' as an adjective or adverb is used in conjunction with both the natural and social sciences, and refers to the use of working hypotheses that are testable using observation or experiment.
    a. EmpiriCal
    b. A Mathematical Theory of Communication
    c. A posteriori
    d. A chemical equation

6. _____ or experimental probability, is the ratio of the number favorable outcomes to the total number of trials, not in a sample space but in an actual sequence of experiments. In a more general sense, _____ estimates probabilities from experience and observation. The phrase a posteriori probability has also been used an alternative to _____ or relative frequency.
    a. A posteriori
    b. EmpiriCal probability
    c. A chemical equation
    d. A Mathematical Theory of Communication

7. In mathematics and physics, there are a _____ number of topics named in honor of Leonhard Euler. As well, many of these topics include their own unique function, equation, formula, identity, number, or other mathematical entity. Unfortunately however, many of these entities have been given simple names like Euler's function, Euler's equation, and Euler's formula, which are further confused by variations of the 'Euler'-prefix Overall though, Euler's work touched upon so many fields that he is often the earliest written reference on a given matter.
    a. Large
    b. List of trigonometry topics
    c. List of integrals of logarithmic functions
    d. List of mathematical knots and links

8. The _____ is a theorem in probability that describes the long-term stability of the mean of a random variable. Given a random variable with a finite expected value, if its values are repeatedly sampled, as the number of these observations increases, their mean will tend to approach and stay close to the expected value.

The LLN can easily be illustrated using the rolls of a die.

a. Random field
b. Graphical model
c. Point process
d. Law of Large Numbers

9. In probability theory and statistics the _____ in favour of an event or a proposition are the quantity p /, where p is the probability of the event or proposition. The _____ against the same event are / p. For example, if you chose a random day of the week, then the _____ that you would choose a Sunday would be 1/6, not 1/7.
   a. Anscombe transform
   b. Event
   c. Odds
   d. Estimation of covariance matrices

10. _____ is a casino and gambling game named after the French word meaning 'small wheel'. In the game, players may choose to place bets on either a number, a range of numbers, the color red or black, or whether the number is odd or even. To determine the winning number and color, a croupier spins a wheel in one direction, then spins a ball in the opposite direction around a tilted circular track running around the circumference of the wheel.
   a. 1-center problem
   b. 2-3 heap
   c. Roulette
   d. 120-cell

11. _____ is the wagering of money or something of material value on an event with an uncertain outcome with the primary intent of winning additional money and/or material goods. Typically, the outcome of the wager is evident within a short period.

The term gaming in this context typically refers to instances in which the activity has been specifically permitted by law.

   a. 120-cell
   b. 2-3 heap
   c. 1-center problem
   d. Gambling

12. _____ or set diagrams are diagrams that show all hypothetically possible logical relations between a finite collection of sets. _____ were invented around 1880 by John Venn. They are used in many fields, including set theory, probability, logic, statistics, and computer science.

Chapter 4. Probability

a. 1-center problem
b. 120-cell
c. 2-3 heap
d. Venn diagrams

13. A _____ is a 2D geometric symbolic representation of information according to some visualization technique. Sometimes, the technique uses a 3D visualization which is then projected onto the 2D surface. The word graph is sometimes used as a synonym for _____.

a. Diagram
b. 2-3 heap
c. 1-center problem
d. 120-cell

14. In simple terms, two events are _____ if they cannot occur at the same time.

In logic, two _____ propositions are propositions that logically cannot both be true. To say that more than two propositions are _____ may, depending on context mean that no two of them can both be true, or only that they cannot all be true.

a. Determinism
b. Philosophy of mathematics
c. Philosophy
d. Mutually exClusive

15. _____ is the probability of some event A, given the occurrence of some other event B. _____ is written P[A | B], and is read 'the probability of A, given B'.

Joint probability is the probability of two events in conjunction. That is, it is the probability of both events together. The joint probability of A and B is written $P(A \cap B)$ or $P(A,B)$.

a. Sample space
b. Quantile
c. Conditional probability
d. Renewal theory

16. _____ is the mathematical operation of scaling one number by another. It is one of the four basic operations in elementary arithmetic.

_____ is defined for whole numbers in terms of repeated addition; for example, 4 multiplied by 3 can be calculated by adding 3 copies of 4 together:

$$4 + 4 + 4 = 12.$$

_____ of rational numbers and real numbers is defined by systematic generalization of this basic idea.

    a. Multiplication
    b. The number 0 is even.
    c. Least common multiple
    d. Highest common factor

17. In set theory, a _____ is a partially ordered set such that for each t ∈ T, the set {s ∈ T : s < t} is well-ordered by the relation <. For each t ∈ T, the order type of {s ∈ T : s < t} is called the height of t. The height of T itself is the least ordinal greater than the height of each element of T.
    a. Tree
    b. Set-theoretic topology
    c. Definable numbers
    d. Transitive reduction

18. In several fields of mathematics the term _____ is used with different but closely related meanings. They all relate to the notion of mapping the elements of a set to other elements of the same set, i.e., exchanging elements of a set.

The general concept of _____ can be defined more formally in different contexts:

In combinatorics, a _____ is usually understood to be a sequence containing each element from a finite set once, and only once.

    a. Tensor product
    b. Cyclic permutation
    c. Linearly independent
    d. Permutation

19. In mathematics, the _____ of a non-negative integer n, denoted by n!, is the product of all positive integers less than or equal to n. For example,

Chapter 4. Probability

$$5! = 1 \times 2 \times 3 \times 4 \times 5 = 120$$

and

$$6! = 1 \times 2 \times 3 \times 4 \times 5 \times 6 = 720$$

The notation n! was introduced by Christian Kramp in 1808.

The _____ function is formally defined by

$$n! = \prod_{k=1}^{n} k \quad \forall n \in \mathbb{N}.$$

The above definition incorporates the instance

$$0! = 1$$

as an instance of the fact that the product of no numbers at all is 1.

   a. Partition of a set
   b. Plane partition
   c. Symbolic combinatorics
   d. FaCtorial

20. In combinatorial mathematics, a _____ is an un-ordered collection of distinct elements, usually of a prescribed size and taken from a given set. Given such a set S, a _____ of elements of S is just a subset of S, where as always forsets the order of the elements is not taken into account. Also, as always forsets, no elements can be repeated more than once in a _____; this is often referred to as a 'collection without repetition'.
   a. Sparsity
   b. Fill-in
   c. Heawood number
   d. Combination

21. In _____, the probability of many events can be determined by direct calculation In most cases, the probabilities and odds are approximations due to rounding.

a. Poker
b. 1-center problem
c. 2-3 heap
d. 120-cell

22. In probability theory and statistics, the _____ of a random variable is the integral of the random variable with respect to its probability measure. For discrete random variables this is equivalent to the probability-weighted sum of the possible values, and for continuous random variables with a density function it is the probability density-weighted integral of the possible values.

The _____ may be intuitively understood by the law of large numbers: The _____, when it exists, is almost surely the limit of the sample mean as sample size grows to infinity.

a. Infinitely divisible distribution
b. Event
c. Illustration
d. Expected value

23. The _____ is a diagram that is used to predict the outcome of a particular cross or breeding experiment. It is named after Reginald C. Punnett, who devised the approach, and is used by biologists to determine the probability of an offspring having a particular genotype.
a. Hardy-Weinberg principle
b. Significance analysis of microarrays
c. Genetics
d. Punnett square

Chapter 5. Statistics

1. _____ are used to describe the basic features of the data gathered from an experimental study in various ways. A _____ is distinguished from inductive statistics. They provide simple summaries about the sample and the measures.
   a. Failure rate
   b. Biostatistics
   c. Null hypothesis
   d. Descriptive statistics

2. A _____ is the result of applying a function to a set of data.

   More formally, statistical theory defines a _____ as a function of a sample where the function itself is independent of the sample's distribution: the term is used both for the function and for the value of the function on a given sample.

   A _____ is distinct from an unknown statistical parameter, which is not computable from a sample.

   a. Spatial dependence
   b. Parameter space
   c. Loss function
   d. Statistic

3. _____ is a mathematical science pertaining to the collection, analysis, interpretation or explanation, and presentation of data. It also provides tools for prediction and forecasting based on data. It is applicable to a wide variety of academic disciplines, from the natural and social sciences to the humanities, government and business.
   a. Probability distribution
   b. Statistics
   c. Percentile rank
   d. Regression toward the mean

4. In statistics the _____ of an event i is the number n_i of times the event occurred in the experiment or the study. These frequencies are often graphically represented in histograms.

   We speak of absolute frequencies, when the counts n_i themselves are given and of

   $$f_i = \frac{n_i}{N} = \frac{n_i}{\sum_i n_i}$$

   Taking the f_i for all i and tabulating or plotting them leads to a _____ distribution.

Chapter 5. Statistics

   a. Digital room correction
   b. Subharmonic
   c. Frequency
   d. Robinson-Dadson curves

5. In statistics, a _____ is a list of the values that a variable takes in a sample. It is usually a list, ordered by quantity, showing the number of times each value appears. For example, if 100 people rate a five-point Likert scale assessing their agreement with a statement on a scale on which 1 denotes strong agreement and 5 strong disagreement, the _____ of their responses might look like:

This simple tabulation has two drawbacks.

   a. Percentile
   b. Confounding
   c. Covariance
   d. Frequency distribution

6. In differential geometry, a discipline within mathematics, a _____ is a subset of the tangent bundle of a manifold satisfying certain properties. _____s are used to build up notions of integrability, and specifically of a foliation of a manifold
   a. Discontinuity
   b. Constraint
   c. Coherence
   d. Distribution

7. In set theory and its applications throughout mathematics, a _____ is a collection of sets that can be unambiguously defined by a property that all its members share. The precise definition of '_____' depends on foundational context. In work on ZF set theory, the notion of _____ is informal, whereas other set theories, such as NBG set theory, axiomatize the notion of '_____'.
   a. Filter
   b. Coherence
   c. Congruent
   d. Class

8. A bar chart or _____ is a chart with rectangular bars with lengths proportional to the values that they represent. Bar charts are used for comparing two or more values. The bars can be horizontally or vertically oriented.

a. 120-cell
b. 1-center problem
c. Bar graph
d. 2-3 heap

9. In statistics, a _____ is a graphical display of tabulated frequencies, shown as bars. It shows what proportion of cases fall into each of several categories. A _____ differs from a bar chart in that it is the area of the bar that denotes the value, not the height as in bar charts, a crucial distinction when the categories are not of uniform width.

a. Probability distribution
b. Histogram
c. First-hitting-time models
d. Standardized moment

10. A _____ is a circular chart divided into sectors, illustrating relative magnitudes or frequences or percents. In a _____, the arc length of each sector, is proportional to the quantity it represents. Together, the sectors create a full disk.

a. 2-3 heap
b. 1-center problem
c. Pie chart
d. 120-cell

11. _____s are words, phrases and clusters of words and phrases that some people believe are meaningful and exist intentionally in coded form in the text of the Bible. These codes were made famous by the book The _____, which suggests that these codes offer warnings for the future.

Contemporary discussion and controversy around one specific encryption method became widespread in 1994 when Doron Witztum, Eliyahu Rips and Yoav Rosenberg published a paper, 'Equidistant Letter Sequences in the Book of Genesis' in the scientific journal Statistical Science.

a. 120-cell
b. 1-center problem
c. Bible Code
d. GNU Privacy Guard

12. In information theory, a _____ is a function mapping an alphabet to non-negative real numbers, satisfying a generalization of Kraft's inequality. A _____ page, a type of character encoding table, is one such _____.

a. File Camouflage
b. Deterministic encryption
c. Link encryption
d. Code

13. In statistics, the _____ is the value that occurs the most frequently in a data set or a probability distribution. In some fields, notably education, sample data are often called scores, and the sample _____ is known as the modal score.

Like the statistical mean and the median, the _____ is a way of capturing important information about a random variable or a population in a single quantity.

a. Function
b. Field
c. Mode
d. Deltoid

14. In geometry, a _____ of a triangle is a line segment joining a vertex to the midpoint of the opposing side. Every triangle has exactly three _____s; one running from each vertex to the opposite side.

The three _____s are concurrent at a point known as the triangle's centroid, or center of mass of the triangle.

a. Percentile rank
b. Correlation
c. Median
d. Statistical significance

15. In statistics, _____ has two related meanings:

- the arithmetic _____.
- the expected value of a random variable, which is also called the population _____.

It is sometimes stated that the '_____' _____s average. This is incorrect if '_____' is taken in the specific sense of 'arithmetic _____' as there are different types of averages: the _____, median, and mode. For instance, average house prices almost always use the median value for the average.

For a real-valued random variable X, the _____ is the expectation of X.

a. Proportional hazards model
b. Statistical population
c. Probability
d. Mean

16. A _____ is the value of a variable below which a certain percent of observations fall. So the 20th _____ is the value below which 20 percent of the observations may be found. The term _____ and the related term _____ rank are often used in descriptive statistics as well as in the reporting of scores from norm-referenced tests.

a. Statistically significant
b. Logistic regression
c. Percentile
d. Frequency distribution

17. In mathematics and statistics, _____ is a measure of difference for interval and ratio variables between the observed value and the mean. The sign of _____, either positive or negative, indicates whether the observation is larger than or smaller than the mean. The magnitude of the value reports how different an observation is from the mean.

a. Filter
b. Deviation
c. Functional
d. Conchoid

18. In descriptive statistics, the _____ is the length of the smallest interval which contains all the data. It is calculated by subtracting the smallest observations from the greatest and provides an indication of statistical dispersion.

It is measured in the same units as the data.

a. Kernel
b. Range
c. Class
d. Bandwidth

19. In probability and statistics, the _____ is a measure of the dispersion of a collection of numbers. It can apply to a probability distribution, a random variable, a population or a data set. The _____ is usually denoted with the letter σ.

Chapter 5. Statistics

a. Statistical population
b. Null hypothesis
c. Standard deviation
d. Failure rate

20. In mathematics, the concept of a _____ tries to capture the intuitive idea of a geometrical one-dimensional and continuous object. A simple example is the circle. In everyday use of the term '_____', a straight line is not curved, but in mathematical parlance _____s include straight lines and line segments.
    a. Curve
    b. Negative pedal curve
    c. Quadrifolium
    d. Kappa curve

21. In mathematics, specifically in combinatorial commutative algebra, a convex lattice polytope P is called _____ if it has the following property: given any positive integer n, every lattice point of the dilation nP, obtained from P by scaling its vertices by the factor n and taking the convex hull of the resulting points, can be written as the sum of exactly n lattice points in P. This property plays an important role in the theory of toric varieties, where it corresponds to projective normality of the toric variety determined by P.

The simplex in R^k with the vertices at the origin and along the unit coordinate vectors is _____.

   a. Polytetrahedron
   b. Demihypercubes
   c. Hypercube
   d. Normal

22. The _____ is an important family of continuous probability distributions, applicable in many fields. Each member of the family may be defined by two parameters, location and scale: the mean and variance respectively. The standard _____ is the _____ with a mean of zero and a variance of one.
    a. Percentile rank
    b. Null hypothesis
    c. Normal distribution
    d. Coefficient of variation

23. In mathematics, _____ are used in the study of chance and probability. They were developed to assist in the analysis of games of chance, stochastic events, and the results of scientific experiments by capturing only the mathematical properties necessary to answer probabilistic questions. Further formalizations have firmly grounded the entity in the theoretical domains of mathematics by making use of measure theory.

a. Statistics
b. Random variables
c. Median polish
d. Statistical dispersion

24. A _____ is a structured activity, usually undertaken for enjoyment and sometimes also used as an educational tool. _____s are distinct from work, which is usually carried out for remuneration, and from art, which is more concerned with the expression of ideas. However, the distinction is not clear-cut, and many _____s are also considered to be work (such as professional players of spectator sports/_____s) or art (such as jigsaw puzzles or _____s involving an artistic layout such as Mah-jongg solitaire.)
   a. 2-3 heap
   b. 120-cell
   c. 1-center problem
   d. Game

25. _____ is a dimensionless quantity derived by subtracting the population mean from an individual raw score and then dividing the difference by the population standard deviation.
   a. 2-3 heap
   b. 120-cell
   c. 1-center problem
   d. Z-score

26. Following a statistical study, a layman may well ask: 'How much _____ can we have in these conclusions?'. A problem immediately arises because a statistician's technical understanding of the term '_____' can differ radically from a layperson's.

The question 'how much _____ can we have in these conclusions?' can have several ramifications, some of which are:

- how reliable are the individual items of data being analysed: do the values measure what they are supposed to measure?
- how extensive is the dataset?
- how representative of the target population is the sample selected?
- how accurately can the important quantities be estimated from the dataset?
- if testing that an intervention has an effect, what is the smallest size of effect that could reliably have been detected from such a dataset as was available.

The last two questions correspond broadly to outcomes of statistical analyses using _____ intervals and examining the statistical power of a test, but careful interpretation is needed. Other statistical approches to these questions are available.

a. Confidence
b. 2-3 heap
c. 1-center problem
d. 120-cell

27. In statistics, a _____ or confidence bound is an interval estimate of a population parameter. Instead of estimating the parameter by a single value, an interval likely to include the parameter is given. Thus, _____s are used to indicate the reliability of an estimate.

a. Time series
b. Kurtosis
c. Percentile rank
d. Confidence interval

28. In mathematics, a _____ is a set of real numbers with the property that any number that lies between two numbers in the set is also included in the set. For example, the set of all numbers x satisfying $0 \leq x \leq 1$ is an _____ which contains 0 and 1, as well as all numbers between them. Other examples of _____s are the set of all real numbers $\mathbb{R}$, the set of all positive real numbers, and the empty set.

a. Annihilator
b. Interval
c. Ideal
d. Order

29. The _____ states that the re-averaged sum of a sufficiently large number of identically distributed independent random variables each with finite mean and variance will be approximately normally distributed . Formally, a _____ is any of a set of weak-convergence results in probability theory. They all express the fact that any sum of many independent identically distributed random variables will tend to be distributed according to a particular 'attractor distribution'.

a. Conditional probability
b. Central Limit Theorem
c. Probability interpretations
d. Regular conditional probability

Chapter 5. Statistics

30. In mathematics, the concept of a '_____' is used to describe the behavior of a function as its argument or input either 'gets close' to some point, or as the argument becomes arbitrarily large; or the behavior of a sequence's elements as their index increases indefinitely. _____s are used in calculus and other branches of mathematical analysis to define derivatives and continuity.

In formulas, _____ is usually abbreviated as lim.

a. Duality
b. Contact
c. Copula
d. Limit

31. In statistics, a _____ is a subset of a population. Typically, the population is very large, making a census or a complete enumeration of all the values in the population impractical or impossible. The _____ represents a subset of manageable size.

a. Duality
b. Boussinesq approximation
c. Dispersion
d. Sample

32. _____ and sample covariance are statistics computed from a collection of data, thought of as being random.

Given a random sample $X_1, \ldots, X_N$ from an n-dimensional random variable X, the _____ is

$$\bar{X} = \frac{1}{N} \sum_{k=1}^{N} X_k.$$

In coordinates, writing the vectors as columns,

$$X_k = \begin{bmatrix} x_{1k} \\ \vdots \\ x_{nk} \end{bmatrix}, \quad \bar{X} = \begin{bmatrix} \bar{x}_1 \\ \vdots \\ \bar{x}_n \end{bmatrix},$$

the entries of the _____ are

$$\bar{x}_i = \frac{1}{N} \sum_{k=1}^{N} x_{ik}, \quad i = 1, \ldots, n.$$

The sample covariance of $X_1, \ldots, X_N$ is the n-by-n matrix $Q = [q_{ij}]$ with the entries given by

$$q_{ij} = \frac{1}{N-1} \sum_{k=1}^{N} (x_{ik} - \bar{x}_i)(x_{jk} - \bar{x}_j)$$

The _____ and the sample covariance matrix are unbiased estimates of the mean and the covariance matrix of the random variable X. The reason why the sample covariance matrix has $N - 1$ in the denominator rather than N is essentially that the population mean E is not known and is replaced by the _____ $\bar{x}$.

a. Sample mean
b. Covariance
c. Mathematical statistics
d. Skewness

33. In mathematics, a _____ is a statement that can be proved on the basis of explicitly stated or previously agreed assumptions.
    a. Disjunction introduction
    b. Theorem
    c. Logical value
    d. Boolean function

34. The _____ is a statistic expressing the amount of random sampling error in a survey's results. The larger the _____, the less faith one should have that the poll's reported results are close to the 'true' figures; that is, the figures for the whole population.

The _____ is usually defined as the 'radius' of a confidence interval for a particular statistic from a survey.

a. Margin of error
b. Squared deviations
c. Conditional variance
d. Moment about the mean

35. In probability theory and statistics, the _____, named after Swiss scientist Jakob Bernoulli, is a discrete probability distribution, which takes value 1 with success probability p and value 0 with failure probability q = 1 − p. So if X is a random variable with this distribution, we have:

$$\Pr(X = 1) = 1 - \Pr(X = 0) = 1 - q = p.$$

The probability mass function f of this distribution is

$$f(k;p) = \begin{cases} p & \text{if } k = 1, \\ 1 - p & \text{if } k = 0, \\ 0 & \text{otherwise.} \end{cases}$$

This can also be expressed as

$$f(k;p) = p^k(1-p)^{1-k}.$$

The expected value of a Bernoulli random variable X is $E(X) = p$, and its variance is

$$\text{var}(X) = p(1-p).$$

The kurtosis goes to infinity for high and low values of p, but for p = 1/2 the _____ has a lower kurtosis than any other probability distribution, namely -2.

a. Correlation
b. Meta-analysis
c. Sample mean
d. Bernoulli distribution

36. In statistics, _____ is a method of sampling from a population.

When sub-populations vary considerably, it is advantageous to sample each subpopulation independently. Stratification is the process of grouping members of the population into relatively homogeneous subgroups before sampling.

a. Stratified sampling
b. Sampling distribution
c. Geometric mean
d. Linear regression

37. In signal processing, _____ is the reduction of a continuous signal to a discrete signal. A common example is the conversion of a sound wave to a sequence of samples.

A sample refers to a value or set of values at a point in time and/or space.

   a. Disk
   b. Sampling
   c. Decidable
   d. Converse logic

Chapter 6. Paths and Networks

1. In geometry, a _____ is a special kind of point, usually a corner of a polygon, polyhedron, or higher dimensional polytope. In the geometry of curves a _____ is a point of where the first derivative of curvature is zero. In graph theory, a _____ is the fundamental unit out of which graphs are formed
    a. Duality
    b. Dini
    c. Crib
    d. Vertex

2. A _____ is a structure built to span a gorge, valley, road, railroad track, river, body of water for the purpose of providing passage over the obstacle. Designs of _____s will vary depending on the function of the _____ and the nature of the terrain where the _____ is to be constructed. Roman _____ of Córdoba, Spain, built in the 1st century BC. Ponte di Pietra in Verona, Italy. A log _____ in the French Alps near Vallorcine. An English 18th century example of a _____ in the Palladian style, with shops on the span: Pulteney _____, Bath A Han Dynasty Chinese miniature model of two residential towers joined by a _____

The first _____s were made by nature -- as simple as a log fallen across a stream.

   a. 1-center problem
   b. 2-3 heap
   c. Bridge
   d. 120-cell

3. The word _____ has many distinct meanings in different fields of knowledge, depending on their methodologies and the context of discussion. Broadly speaking we can say that a _____ is some kind of belief or claim that (supposedly) explains, asserts, or consolidates some class of claims. Additionally, in contrast with a theorem the statement of the _____ is generally accepted only in some tentative fashion as opposed to regarding it as having been conclusively established.
    a. Theory
    b. Defined
    c. Transport of structure
    d. Per mil

4. In graph theory, a _____ is an edge that connects a vertex to itself. A simple graph contains no _____s.

Chapter 6. Paths and Networks

Depending on the context, a graph or a multigraph may be defined so as to either allow or disallow the presence of _____s:

- Where graphs are defined so as to allow _____s and multiple edges, a graph without _____s is often called a multigraph.
- Where graphs are defined so as to disallow _____s and multiple edges, a multigraph or a pseudograph is often defined to mean a 'graph' which can have _____s and multiple edges.

For an undirected graph, the degree of a vertex is equal to the number of adjacent vertices.

A special case is a _____, which adds two to the degree.

   a. Commensurable
   b. FISH
   c. Duality
   d. Loop

5. In graph theory, a _____ in a graph is a sequence of vertices such that from each of its vertices there is an edge to the next vertex in the sequence. The first vertex is called the start vertex and the last vertex is called the end vertex. Both of them are called end or terminal vertices of the _____.
   a. Blinding
   b. Deltoid
   c. Class
   d. Path

6. In graph theory, an _____ is a path in a graph which visits each edge exactly once. Similarly, an Eulerian circuit is an _____ which starts and ends on the same vertex. They were first discussed by Leonhard Euler while solving the famous Seven Bridges of Königsberg problem in 1736.
   a. Eulerian path
   b. Independent set
   c. Adjacent vertex
   d. Isomorphism of graphs

7. The _____ states that given any plane separated into regions, such as a political map of the states of a country, the regions may be colored using no more than four colors in such a way that no two adjacent regions receive the same color. Two regions are called adjacent only if they share a border segment, not just a point. Each region must be contiguous: that is, it may not have exclaves like some real countries such as Angola, Azerbaijan, Italy, the United States, or Russia.

Chapter 6. Paths and Networks

a. Strong coloring
b. Four Color Theorem
c. Subcoloring
d. Total coloring

8. In mathematics, a _____ is a statement that can be proved on the basis of explicitly stated or previously agreed assumptions.
   a. Theorem
   b. Boolean function
   c. Disjunction introduction
   d. Logical value

9. In mathematics and computer science, _____ is the study of graphs: mathematical structures used to model pairwise relations between objects from a certain collection. A 'graph' in this context refers to a collection of vertices or 'nodes' and a collection of edges that connect pairs of vertices. A graph may be undirected, meaning that there is no distinction between the two vertices associated with each edge, or its edges may be directed from one vertex to another; see graph for more detailed definitions and for other variations in the types of graphs that are commonly considered.
   a. Partial equivalence relation
   b. Pooling design
   c. Discrete mathematics
   d. Graph theory

10. In graph theory, a branch of mathematics, the _____, postman tour or route inspection problem is to find a shortest closed trail that visits every edge of a undirected graph. When the graph has an Eulerian circuit, that circuit is an optimal solution.

    Alan Goldman of NIST first coined the name '_____' for this problem, as it was originally studied by the Chinese mathematician Mei-Ku Kuan in 1962.

    a. Liquid schedule
    b. Bottleneck traveling salesman
    c. Chinese postman problem
    d. Bipartite dimension

11. In the mathematical field of graph theory, a _____ is a path in an undirected graph which visits each vertex exactly once. A Hamiltonian cycle is a cycle in an undirected graph which visits each vertex exactly once and also returns to the starting vertex. Determining whether such paths and cycles exist in graphs is the _____ problem which is NP-complete.

Chapter 6. Paths and Networks

a. Complex network
b. Graceful labeling
c. Centrality
d. Hamiltonian path

12. In the physical sciences, _____ is a measurement of the gravitational force acting on an object. Near the surface of the Earth, the acceleration due to gravity is approximately constant; this means that an object's _____ is roughly proportional to its mass.

In commerce and in many other applications, _____ means the same as mass as that term is used in physics.

a. 2-3 heap
b. Weight
c. 120-cell
d. 1-center problem

13. In mathematical analysis, a metric space M is said to be _____ (or Cauchy) if every Cauchy sequence of points in M has a limit that is also in M or alternatively if every Cauchy sequence in M converges in M.

Intuitively, a space is _____ if there are no 'points missing' from it (inside or at the boundary.) For instance, the set of rational numbers is not _____, because $\sqrt{2}$ is 'missing' from it, even though one can construct a Cauchy sequence of rational numbers that converges to it.

a. 1-center problem
b. 2-3 heap
c. 120-cell
d. Complete

14. In the mathematical field of graph theory, a _____ is a simple graph in which every pair of distinct vertices is connected by an edge. The _____ on n vertices has n vertices and n edges, and is denoted by K_n. It is a regular graph of degree n − 1.

a. Wheel graph
b. Complete graph
c. 120-cell
d. 1-center problem

Chapter 6. Paths and Networks

15. The _____ in operations research is a problem in discrete or combinatorial optimization. It is a prominent illustration of a class of problems in computational complexity theory which are classified as NP-hard.

The problem is: given a number of cities and the costs of travelling from any city to any other city, what is the least-cost round-trip route that visits each city exactly once and then returns to the starting city?

Given a number of cities and the costs of travelling from any city to any other city, what is the least-cost round-trip route that visits each city exactly once and then returns to the starting city?

The size of the solution space is!/2 for n > 2, where n is the number of cities.

a. New digraph reconstruction conjecture
b. Snake-in-the-box
c. Cut vertex
d. Travelling salesman problem

16. In mathematics, computing, linguistics and related subjects, an _____ is a sequence of finite instructions, often used for calculation and data processing. It is formally a type of effective method in which a list of well-defined instructions for completing a task will, when given an initial state, proceed through a well-defined series of successive states, eventually terminating in an end-state. The transition from one state to the next is not necessarily deterministic; some _____s, known as probabilistic _____s, incorporate randomness.

a. Approximate counting algorithm
b. In-place algorithm
c. Out-of-core
d. Algorithm

17. A _____ is any algorithm that follows the problem solving metaheuristic of making the locally optimum choice at each stage with the hope of finding the global optimum.

For example, applying the greedy strategy to the traveling salesman problem yields the following algorithm: 'At each stage visit the unvisited city nearest to the current city'.

In general, _____s have five pillars:

1. A candidate set, from which a solution is created
2. A selection function, which chooses the best candidate to be added to the solution
3. A feasibility function, that is used to determine if a candidate can be used to contribute to a solution
4. An objective function, which assigns a value to a solution, or a partial solution, and
5. A solution function, which will indicate when we have discovered a complete solution

_____s produce good solutions on some mathematical problems, but not on others. Most problems for which they work well have two properties:

Greedy choice property
      We can make whatever choice seems best at the moment and then solve the subproblems that arise later.

    a. Simplex method
    b. Differential evolution
    c. Fibonacci search
    d. Greedy algorithm

18. In optimization, the _____ algorithm is one of the best heuristics for the Euclidean traveling salesman problem. It briefly involves swapping pairs of sub-tours to make a new tour. It is a generalization of 2-opt and 3-opt.
    a. Wing shape optimization
    b. Distributed constraint optimization
    c. Quadratic programming
    d. Lin-Kernighan

19. In the mathematical field of graph theory, a _____ T of a connected, undirected graph G is a tree composed of all the vertices and some of the edges of G. Informally, a _____ of G is a selection of edges of G that form a tree spanning every vertex. That is, every vertex lies in the tree, but no cycles are formed.
    a. Spanning tree
    b. Chord
    c. Lattice
    d. Germ

20. In set theory, a _____ is a partially ordered set such that for each $t \in T$, the set $\{s \in T : s < t\}$ is well-ordered by the relation <. For each $t \in T$, the order type of $\{s \in T : s < t\}$ is called the height of t. The height of T itself is the least ordinal greater than the height of each element of T.
    a. Transitive reduction
    b. Set-theoretic topology
    c. Definable numbers
    d. Tree

21. A _____ is a structured activity, usually undertaken for enjoyment and sometimes also used as an educational tool. _____s are distinct from work, which is usually carried out for remuneration, and from art, which is more concerned with the expression of ideas. However, the distinction is not clear-cut, and many _____s are also considered to be work (such as professional players of spectator sports/_____s) or art (such as jigsaw puzzles or _____s involving an artistic layout such as Mah-jongg solitaire.)
   a. Game
   b. 2-3 heap
   c. 1-center problem
   d. 120-cell

Chapter 7. Tilings and Polyhedra

1. In geometry a _____ is traditionally a plane figure that is bounded by a closed path or circuit, composed of a finite sequence of straight line segments. These segments are called its edges or sides, and the points where two edges meet are the _____'s vertices or corners. The interior of the _____ is sometimes called its body.
    a. Parallelogon
    b. Polygon
    c. Polygonal curve
    d. Regular polygon

2. In geometry, a _____ is a special kind of point, usually a corner of a polygon, polyhedron, or higher dimensional polytope. In the geometry of curves a _____ is a point of where the first derivative of curvature is zero. In graph theory, a _____ is the fundamental unit out of which graphs are formed
    a. Duality
    b. Crib
    c. Vertex
    d. Dini

3. In abstract algebra, a module S over a ring R is called _____ or irreducible if it is not the zero module 0 and if its only submodules are 0 and S. Understanding the _____ modules over a ring is usually helpful because these modules form the 'building blocks' of all other modules in a certain sense.

Abelian groups are the same as Z-modules.

    a. Basis
    b. Simple
    c. Harmonic series
    d. Derivation

4. In geometry, a _____ is a polygon whose sides do not intersect. They are also called Jordan polygons, because the Jordan curve theorem can be used to prove that such a polygon divides the plane into two regions, the region inside it and the region outside it. A _____ is topologically equivalent to a disk.
    a. Regular decagon
    b. Simple Polygon
    c. Regular octagon
    d. Star-shaped polygon

5. In mathematics, a real-valued function f defined on an interval is called _____, concave upwards, concave up or _____ cup, if for any two points x and y in its domain C and any t in [0,1], we have

$$f(tx + (1-t)y) \leq tf(x) + (1-t)f(y).$$

_____ function on an interval.

In other words, a function is _____ if and only if its epigraph is a _____ set.

Pictorially, a function is called '_____' if the function lies below the straight line segment connecting two points, for any two points in the interval.

A function is called strictly _____ if

$$f(tx + (1-t)y) < tf(x) + (1-t)f(y)$$

for any t in and $x \neq y$.

A function f is said to be concave if − f is _____.

a. Convex
b. Contrapositive
c. Continuum
d. Continuous wavelet

6. In geometry, a polygon can be either convex or concave.

A _____ is a simple polygon whose interior is a convex set. The following properties of a simple polygon are all equivalent to convexity:

- Every internal angle is less than 180 degrees or equal to 180 degrees.
- Every line segment between two vertices of the polygon does not go exterior to the polygon.

A simple polygon is strictly convex if every internal angle is strictly less than 180 degrees. Equivalently, a polygon is strictly convex if every line segment between two nonadjacent vertices of the polygon is strictly interior to the polygon except at its endpoints.

a. Convex polygon
b. Continuous phase modulation
c. Charles's Law
d. Claw-free permutations

Chapter 7. Tilings and Polyhedra

7. In geometry and trigonometry, an _____ is the figure formed by two rays sharing a common endpoint, called the vertex of the _____. The magnitude of the _____ is the 'amount of rotation' that separates the two rays, and can be measured by considering the length of circular arc swept out when one ray is rotated about the vertex to coincide with the other. Where there is no possibility of confusion, the term '_____' is used interchangeably for both the geometric configuration itself and for its angular magnitude.
   a. A posteriori
   b. A Mathematical Theory of Communication
   c. A chemical equation
   d. Angle

8. A _____ is a polygon which is equiangular and equilateral. _____s may be convex or star.

These properties apply to both convex and star _____s.

   a. Constructible polygon
   b. Regular decagon
   c. Regular polygon
   d. Star-shaped polygon

9. A _____ or tiling of the plane is a collection of plane figures that fills the plane with no overlaps and no gaps. One may also speak of _____s of the parts of the plane or of other surfaces. Generalizations to higher dimensions are also possible.
   a. Symmetry breaking
   b. Tessellation
   c. Directional symmetry
   d. Molecular symmetry

10. A _____ is often defined as a geometric object with flat faces and straight edges.

This definition of a _____ is not very precise, and to a modern mathematician is quite unsatisfactory. Grünbaum observed that:

The Original Sin in the theory of polyhedra goes back to Euclid, and through Kepler, Poinsot, Cauchy and many others ...

a. 2-3 heap
b. 1-center problem
c. 120-cell
d. Polyhedron

11. In mathematics, a _____ is a statement that can be proved on the basis of explicitly stated or previously agreed assumptions.
   a. Boolean function
   b. Disjunction introduction
   c. Theorem
   d. Logical value

12. A _____ is a nonperiodic tiling generated by an aperiodic set of prototiles named after Roger Penrose, who investigated these sets in the 1970s. Because all tilings obtained with the Penrose tiles are non-periodic, _____s are considered aperiodic tilings. Among the infinitely many possible tilings there are two that possess both mirror symmetry and fivefold rotational symmetry, as in the diagram at the right, and the term _____ usually refers to them.
   a. Penrose tiling
   b. 120-cell
   c. 2-3 heap
   d. 1-center problem

13. The informal term _____ loosely refers to an aperiodic set of tiles and the tilings which such sets admit. Properly speaking, aperiodicity is a property of the set of tiles themselves; a given tiling is simply non-periodic or periodic. Further confusing the matter is that a given aperiodic set of tiles typically admits infinitely many distinct tilings.
   a. Uniform tiling
   b. A Mathematical Theory of Communication
   c. Unstructured grid
   d. Aperiodic Tiling

14. The term _____ refers to the central sense organ complex, for those animals that have one, normally on the ventral surface of the head and can depending on the definition in the human case, include the hair, forehead, eyebrow, eyes, nose, ears, cheeks, mouth, lips, philtrum, teeth, skin, and chin. The _____ has uses of expression, appearance, and identity amongst others.It also has different senses like smelling, tasting, hearing, and seeing.

Chapter 7. Tilings and Polyhedra

Caricatures often exaggerate facial features to make a _____ more easily recognized in association with a pronounced portion of the _____ of the individual in question--for example, a caricature of Osama bin Laden might focus on his facial hair and nose; a caricature of George W. Bush might enlarge his ears to the size of an elephant¢s; a caricature of Jay Leno may pronounce his head and chin; and a caricature of Mick Jagger might enlarge his lips.

a. 2-3 heap
b. 120-cell
c. 1-center problem
d. FaCe

15. In mathematics and in the sciences, a _____ (plural: _____e, formulæ or _____s) is a concise way of expressing information symbolically (as in a mathematical or chemical _____), or a general relationship between quantities. One of many famous _____e is Albert Einstein's E = mc² (see special relativity

In mathematics, a _____ is a key to solve an equation with variables. For example, the problem of determining the volume of a sphere is one that requires a significant amount of integral calculus to solve.

a. 1-center problem
b. 2-3 heap
c. 120-cell
d. Formula

16. In geometry, a _____ is a convex regular polyhedron. These are the three-dimensional analogs of the convex regular polygons. There are precisely five such figures.
a. 120-cell
b. 2-3 heap
c. 1-center problem
d. Platonic solid

17. _____ are small polyhedral objects, usually cubic, used for generating random numbers or other symbols. This makes _____ suitable as gambling devices, especially for craps or sic bo, or for use in non-gambling tabletop games.

A traditional die is a cube, marked on each of its six faces with a different number of circular patches or pits called pips.

a. 2-3 heap
b. Dice
c. 1-center problem
d. 120-cell

18. An n-sided _____ is a polyhedron composed of two parallel copies of some particular n-sided polygon, connected by an alternating band of triangles. _____s are a subclass of the prismatoids.

_____s are similar to prisms except the bases are twisted relative to each other, and that the side faces are triangles, rather than quadrilaterials.

a. Antiprism
b. A Mathematical Theory of Communication
c. A chemical equation
d. A posteriori

19. In geometry an _____ is a highly symmetric, semi-regular convex polyhedron composed of two or more types of regular polygons meeting in identical vertices. They are distinct from the Platonic solids, which are composed of only one type of polygon meeting in identical vertices, and from the Johnson solids, whose regular polygonal faces do not meet in identical vertices. The symmetry of the _____s excludes the members of the dihedral group, the prisms and antiprisms.

a. A chemical equation
b. A posteriori
c. ArChimedean solid
d. A Mathematical Theory of Communication

Chapter 8. Number Theory

1. A _____ number is a positive integer which has a positive divisor other than one or itself. By definition, every integer greater than one is either a prime number or a _____ number. zero and one are considered to be neither prime nor _____. For example, the integer 14 is a _____ number because it can be factored as 2 × 7.
   a. Key server
   b. Basis
   c. Composite
   d. Discontinuity

2. A _____ is a positive integer which has a positive divisor other than one or itself. In other words, if 0 < n is an integer and there are integers 1 < a, b < n such that n = a × b then n is composite. By definition, every integer greater than one is either a prime number or a _____.
   a. Prime Pages
   b. Ruth-Aaron pair
   c. Megaprime
   d. Composite number

3. In mathematics, a _____ of an integer n is an integer which evenly divides n without leaving a remainder.

   For example, 7 is a _____ of 42 because 42/7 = 6. We also say 42 is divisible by 7 or 42 is a multiple of 7 or 7 divides 42 or 7 is a factor of 42 and we usually write 7 | 42.

   a. 2-3 heap
   b. 1-center problem
   c. 120-cell
   d. Divisor

4. In number theory, the _____ states that every natural number greater than 1 can be written as a unique product of prime numbers. For instance,

$$6936 = 2^3 \times 3 \times 17^2,$$

$$1200 = 2^4 \times 3 \times 5^2.$$

There are no other possible factorizations of 6936 or 1200 into non-negative prime numbers. The above representation collapses repeated prime factors into powers for easier identification.

a. Fundamental Theorem of Arithmetic
b. Dedekind sums
c. Cyclic number
d. Feit–Thompson theorem

5. The _____ are the set of numbers consisting of the natural numbers including 0 and their negatives. They are numbers that can be written without a fractional or decimal component, and fall within the set {... −2, −1, 0, 1, 2, ...}.

a. A Mathematical Theory of Communication
b. A chemical equation
c. Integers
d. A posteriori

6. _____ is the branch of pure mathematics concerned with the properties of numbers in general, and integers in particular, as well as the wider classes of problems that arise from their study.

_____ may be subdivided into several fields, according to the methods used and the type of questions investigated.

The term 'arithmetic' is also used to refer to _____.

a. Sociable number
b. Coin problem
c. Goormaghtigh conjecture
d. Number theory

7. In mathematics, a _____ is a natural number which has exactly two distinct natural number divisors: 1 and itself. An infinitude of _____s exists, as demonstrated by Euclid around 300 BC. The first twenty-five _____s are:

2, 3, 5, 7, 11, 13, 17, 19, 23, 29, 31, 37, 41, 43, 47, 53, 59, 61, 67, 71, 73, 79, 83, 89, 97.

a. Pronic number
b. Prime number
c. Perrin number
d. Highly composite number

8. In mathematics, a _____ is a statement that can be proved on the basis of explicitly stated or previously agreed assumptions.

a. Boolean function
b. Logical value
c. Disjunction introduction
d. Theorem

9. In mathematics, _____ is a subfield of analytic number theory that deals with prime numbers and with factorization and divisors. The focus is usually on developing approximate formulas for counting these objects in various contexts. The Prime Number Theorem is a key result in this subject.
   a. Ramanujan tau function
   b. Cyclotomic polynomial
   c. Covering set
   d. Multiplicative Number theory

10. The word _____ has many distinct meanings in different fields of knowledge, depending on their methodologies and the context of discussion. Broadly speaking we can say that a _____ is some kind of belief or claim that (supposedly) explains, asserts, or consolidates some class of claims. Additionally, in contrast with a theorem the statement of the _____ is generally accepted only in some tentative fashion as opposed to regarding it as having been conclusively established.
    a. Theory
    b. Defined
    c. Per mil
    d. Transport of structure

11. In mathematics, the _____ is a simple, ancient algorithm for finding all prime numbers up to a specified integer. It works efficiently for the smaller primes. It was created by Eratosthenes, an ancient Greek mathematician.
    a. 120-cell
    b. 2-3 heap
    c. 1-center problem
    d. Sieve of Eratosthenes

12. In mathematics, a _____ is a positive integer of the form

$$F_n = 2^{2^n} + 1$$

where n is a nonnegative integer. The first nine _____s are (sequence A000215 in OEIS):

As of 2008, only F_0 to F_{11} have been completely factored.

If $2^n + 1$ is prime, and $n > 0$, it can be shown that n must be a power of two.

   a. Cabtaxi number
   b. Multiplicative number theory
   c. Q-Vandermonde identity
   d. Fermat number

13. _____ IPA: [pjɛʁ ɛ dɛ™fɛʁ 'ma] (17 August 1601 or 1607/8 - 12 January 1665) was a French lawyer at the Parlement of Toulouse, France, and a mathematician who is given credit for early developments that led to modern calculus. In particular, he is recognized for his discovery of an original method of finding the greatest and the smallest ordinates of curved lines, which is analogous to that of the then unknown differential calculus, as well as his research into the theory of numbers. He also made notable contributions to analytic geometry, probability, and optics.
   a. Pierre de Fermat
   b. Nikita Borisov
   c. Philip J. Davis
   d. Felix Hausdorff

14. In mathematics, computing, linguistics and related subjects, an _____ is a sequence of finite instructions, often used for calculation and data processing. It is formally a type of effective method in which a list of well-defined instructions for completing a task will, when given an initial state, proceed through a well-defined series of successive states, eventually terminating in an end-state. The transition from one state to the next is not necessarily deterministic; some _____s, known as probabilistic _____s, incorporate randomness.
   a. Out-of-core
   b. Approximate counting algorithm
   c. Algorithm
   d. In-place algorithm

15. In mathematics, a _____ is a mathematical statement which appears resourceful, but has not been formally proven to be true under the rules of mathematical logic. Once a _____ is formally proven true it is elevated to the status of theorem and may be used afterwards without risk in the construction of other formal mathematical proofs. Until that time, mathematicians may use the _____ on a provisional basis, but any resulting work is itself provisional until the underlying _____ is cleared up.
   a. Whitehead conjecture
   b. Moral certainty
   c. Conjecture
   d. Heawood conjecture

Chapter 8. Number Theory

16. In mathematics, a _____ is the end result of a division problem. It can also be expressed as the number of times the divisor divides into the dividend.
    a. Marginal cost
    b. Limiting
    c. Quotient
    d. Notation

17. In mathematics, the _____, sometimes known as the greatest common factor or highest common factor, of two non-zero integers, is the largest positive integer that divides both numbers without remainder.

    This notion can be extended to polynomials, see _____ of two polynomials.

    The _____ of a and b is written as gc, or sometimes simply as.

    a. Highest common factor
    b. Greatest common divisor
    c. Minuend
    d. Multiplication

18. In number theory, the _____ is an algorithm to determine the greatest common divisor of two elements of any Euclidean domain. Its major significance is that it does not require factoring the two integers, and it is also significant in that it is one of the oldest algorithms known, dating back to the ancient Greeks.

    The _____ is one of the oldest algorithms known, since it appeared in Euclid's Elements around 300 BC.

    a. A posteriori
    b. A Mathematical Theory of Communication
    c. A chemical equation
    d. EuClidean algorithm

19. In mathematics, in the realm of group theory, a group is said to be _____ if it equals its own commutator subgroup if the group has no nontrivial abelian quotients.

    The smallest _____ group is the alternating group A_5. More generally, any non-abelian simple group is _____ since the commutator subgroup is a normal subgroup with abelian quotient.

Chapter 8. Number Theory 51

a. Quaternion group
b. Free product
c. PerfeCt
d. Group of Lie type

20. In mathematics, a _____ is defined as a positive integer which is the sum of its proper positive divisors, that is, the sum of the positive divisors excluding the number itself. Equivalently, a _____ is a number that is half the sum of all of its positive divisors, or = 2n.

The first _____ is 6, because 1, 2, and 3 are its proper positive divisors, and 1 + 2 + 3 = 6.

a. Leonardo numbers
b. Blum integer
c. Nonhypotenuse number
d. PerfeCt number

21. In mathematics, _____ is a system of arithmetic for integers, where numbers 'wrap around' after they reach a certain value -- the modulus. _____ was introduced by Carl Friedrich Gauss in his book Disquisitiones Arithmeticae, published in 1801.

A familiar use of _____ is its use in the 24-hour clock: the arithmetic of time-keeping in which the day runs from midnight to midnight and is divided into 24 hours, numbered from 0 to 23.

a. Residue number system
b. Discrete logarithm
c. Multiplicative group of integers modulo n
d. Modular arithmetic

22. The word _____ is the Latin ablative of modulus which itself means 'a small measure.' It was introduced into mathematics in the book Disquisitiones Arithmeticae by Carl Friedrich Gauss in 1801. Ever since, however, '_____' has gained many meanings, some exact and some imprecise.

- (This usage is from Gauss's book.) Given the integers a, b and n, the expression a ≡ b (mod n) means that a − b is a multiple of n, or equivalently, a and b both leave the same remainder when divided by n. For more details, see modular arithmetic.

- In computing, given two numbers (either integer or real), a and n, a _____ n is the remainder after numerical division of a by n, under certain constraints. See _____ operation.

a. Per mil
b. Quotition
c. Predictor-corrector method
d. Modulo

23. In geometry, two sets of points are called _____ if one can be transformed into the other by an isometry. Less formally, two figures are _____ if they have the same shape and size, but are in different positions.

In a Euclidean system, congruence is fundamental; it is the counterpart of equality for numbers.

a. Congruent
b. Function
c. Gamma test
d. Germ

24. _____ is a sanity check to ensure that hand computations of sums, differences, products, and quotients of integers are correct. By looking at the digital roots of the inputs and outputs, the casting-out-nines method can help one check arithmetic calculations. The method is so simple that most schoolchildren can apply it without understanding its mathematical underpinnings.

a. Casting out nines
b. Rounding
c. Galley method
d. Tetration

25. A _____ is a form of redundancy check used for error detection, the decimal equivalent of a binary checksum. It consists of a single digit computed from the other digits in the message.

With a _____, one can detect simple errors in the input of a series of digits, such as a single mistyped digit, or the permutation of two successive digits.

a. Forward error correction
b. Data scrubbing
c. Summation check
d. Check digit

Chapter 8. Number Theory

26. The _____ is a unique, numerical commercial book identifier, based upon the 9-digit Standard Book Numbering code created in the UK by the booksellers and stationers W.H. Smith and others in 1966. The 10-digit _____ format was developed by the International Organization for Standardization and published as an international standard, ISO 2108, in 1970. Currently, the ISO TC 46/SC 9 is responsible for the standard.
    a. A Mathematical Theory of Communication
    b. ISBN
    c. A posteriori
    d. A chemical equation

27. In mathematics, an _____ in the sense of ring theory is a subring $\mathcal{O}$ of a ring R that satisfies the conditions

    1. R is a ring which is a finite-dimensional algebra over the rational number field $\mathbb{Q}$
    2. $\mathcal{O}$ spans R over $\mathbb{Q}$, so that $\mathbb{Q}\mathcal{O} = R$, and
    3. $\mathcal{O}$ is a lattice in R.

    The third condition can be stated more accurately, in terms of the extension of scalars of R to the real numbers, embedding R in a real vector space. In less formal terms, additively $\mathcal{O}$ should be a free abelian group generated by a basis for R over $\mathbb{Q}$.

    The leading example is the case where R is a number field K and $\mathcal{O}$ is its ring of integers. In algebraic number theory there are examples for any K other than the rational field of proper subrings of the ring of integers that are also _____s.

    a. Order
    b. Algebraic
    c. Efficiency
    d. Annihilator

28. In informal language, a _____ is a function that swaps two elements of a set. More formally, given a finite set $X = \{a_1, a_2, \ldots, a_n\}$, a _____ is a permutation f, such that there exist indices i,j such that fj, fi and fk for all other indices k. This is often denoted as

For example, if X = {a,b,c,d,e}, the function σ given by

$$\sigma(a) = a$$
$$\sigma(b) = e$$
$$\sigma(c) = c$$
$$\sigma(d) = d$$
$$\sigma(e) = b$$

is a _____.

Any permutation can be expressed as the composition of _____s.

  a. Chiral
  b. C-35
  c. Bounded
  d. Transposition

29. In information theory, a _____ is a function mapping an alphabet to non-negative real numbers, satisfying a generalization of Kraft's inequality. A _____ page, a type of character encoding table, is one such _____.
  a. Deterministic encryption
  b. File Camouflage
  c. Link encryption
  d. Code

30. The _____ is a barcode symbology, that is widely used in the United States and Canada for tracking trade items in stores. In the _____-A barcode, each digit is represented by a seven-bit sequence, encoded by a series of alternating bars and spaces. Guard bars, shown in green, separate the two groups of six digits.

The _____ encodes 12 decimal digits as SLLLLLLMRRRRRRE, where S and E are the bit pattern 101, M is the bit pattern 01010, and each L and R are digits, each one represented by a seven-bit code.

  a. A chemical equation
  b. A Mathematical Theory of Communication
  c. A posteriori
  d. Universal Product Code

Chapter 8. Number Theory

31. A _____ is a competition involving a relatively large number of competitors, all participating in a sport or game. More specifically, the term may be used in either of two overlapping senses:

   1. One or more competitions held at a single venue and concentrated into a relatively short time interval. Some game clubs focus on preparing members for such _____s. Chess clubs, for instance, frequently employ similar ranking systems, chess clocks, and etiquette to those used in chess _____s.
   2. A competition involving multiple matches, each involving a subset of the competitors, with the overall _____ winner determined based on the combined results of these individual matches. These are common in those sports and games where each match must involve a small number of competitors: often precisely two, as in most team sports, racket sports and combat sports, many card games and board games, and many forms of competitive debating. Such _____s allow large numbers to compete against each other in spite of the restriction on numbers in a single match.

   These two senses are distinct. All golf _____s meet the first definition, but while match play _____s meet the second, stroke play _____s do not, since there are no distinct matches within the _____. In contrast, football leagues like the Premier League are _____s in the second sense, but not the first, having matches spread across many stadia over a period of up to a year.

   a. 120-cell
   b. Tournament
   c. 2-3 heap
   d. 1-center problem

32. In cryptography, a _____ the shift cipher, Caesar's code or Caesar shift, is one of the simplest and most widely known encryption techniques. It is a type of substitution cipher in which each letter in the plaintext is replaced by a letter some fixed number of positions down the alphabet. For example, with a shift of 3, A would be replaced by D, B would become E, and so on.
   a. Polar coordinate system
   b. Polar coordinate
   c. Caesar cipher
   d. Big bang

33. In cryptography, _____ is the process of transforming information using an algorithm to make it unreadable to anyone except those possessing special knowledge, usually referred to as a key. The result of the process is encrypted information. In many contexts, the word _____ also implicitly refers to the reverse process, decryption, to make the encrypted information readable again.
   a. Encryption
   b. Authenticated encryption
   c. End-to-end encryption
   d. One-time pad

34. In cryptography, _____ is the information which the sender wishes to transmit to the receive. Before the computer era, _____ simply meant text in the language of the communicating parties. Since computers, the definition has been expanded to include not only the electronic representation of text, such as email and word processor documents, but also the computer representation of speech, music, pictures, videos, ATM and credit card transactions, sensor data, and so forth, basically any information which the communicating parties might wish to conceal from others.

   a. Secure SMS Messaging Protocol
   b. Cleartext
   c. Secure Hash Standard
   d. Plaintext

35. In cryptography, a _____ is an algorithm for performing encryption and decryption -- a series of well-defined steps that can be followed as a procedure. An alternative term is encipherment. In non-technical usage, a '_____' is the same thing as a 'code'; however, the concepts are distinct in cryptography.

   a. Cipher
   b. Transmission security
   c. Group key
   d. Polygraphic substitution

36. The _____ is a special case of the more general monoalphabetic substitution cipher. In _____s the encryption function for a letter is e where,

   - a and m are coprime.
   - m is the size of the alphabet.

The decryption function is d− 1 where a $^{-1}$ is the multiplicative inverse of a in the group $\mathbb{Z}_m$

Considering the specific case of encrypting messages in English, there are a total of 286 non-trivial _____s, not counting the trivial Caesar ciphers obtained when a = 1. This lack of variety renders the system as highly insecure when considered in light of Kerckhoffs' Principle. Even without foreknowledge that a text were enciphered with an _____, the ciphertext would have all of the vulnerabilities of ordinary monoalphabetic substitution ciphers.

   a. Atbash
   b. Autokey cipher
   c. Alphabetum Kaldeorum
   d. Affine cipher

37. In mathematics, the _____ of a number n is the number that, when added to n, yields zero. The _____ of n is denoted −n. For example, 7 is −7, because 7 + (−7) = 0, and the _____ of −0.3 is 0.3, because −0.3 + 0.3 = 0.

a. Algebraic structure
b. Arity
c. Associativity
d. Additive inverse

38. In cryptography, a _____ is a tool used to perform a transposition cipher, consisting of a cylinder with a strip of leather wound around it on which is written a message. The ancient Greeks, and the Spartans in particular, are said to have used this cipher to communicate during military campaigns.

The recipient uses a rod of the same diameter on which he wraps the paper to read the message.

a. Nihilist cipher
b. Substitution cipher
c. M-94
d. Scytale

39. In the history of cryptography, 97-shiki Å bun inji-ki or AngÅ ki Taipu-B, codenamed _____ by the United States, was a diplomatic cryptographic machine used by the Japanese Foreign Office just before and during World War II. The machine was an electromechanical stepping-switch device.

The information gained from decryptions was eventually code-named Magic within the US government.

a. CD-57
b. M-209
c. COMSEC
d. PURPLE

40. In statistics the _____ of an event i is the number n_i of times the event occurred in the experiment or the study. These frequencies are often graphically represented in histograms.

We speak of absolute frequencies, when the counts n_i themselves are given and of

$$f_i = \frac{n_i}{N} = \frac{n_i}{\sum_i n_i}$$

Taking the f_i for all i and tabulating or plotting them leads to a _____ distribution.

Chapter 8. Number Theory

a. Robinson-Dadson curves
b. Digital room correction
c. Subharmonic
d. Frequency

41. In classical cryptography, the _____ is a polygraphic substitution cipher based on linear algebra. Invented by Lester S. Hill in 1929, it was the first polygraphic cipher in which it was practical to operate on more than three symbols at once.
   a. Playfair cipher
   b. Hill cipher
   c. Nihilist cipher
   d. Transposition cipher

42. _____ is an Israeli cryptographer. He was one of the inventors of the RSA algorithm, one of the inventors of the Feige-Fiat-Shamir Identification Scheme, one of the inventors of differential cryptanalysis and has made numerous contributions to the fields of cryptography and computer science.

   Born in Tel Aviv, Shamir received a BS in Mathematics from Tel Aviv University in 1973 and obtained his MSc and PhD in Computer Science from the Weizmann Institute in 1975 and 1977 respectively.

   a. Iain S. Duff
   b. Edwin Thompson Jaynes
   c. Ernst Friedrich Ferdinand Zermelo
   d. Adi Shamir

43. In mathematics and computer science, _____ is the study of graphs: mathematical structures used to model pairwise relations between objects from a certain collection. A 'graph' in this context refers to a collection of vertices or 'nodes' and a collection of edges that connect pairs of vertices. A graph may be undirected, meaning that there is no distinction between the two vertices associated with each edge, or its edges may be directed from one vertex to another; see graph for more detailed definitions and for other variations in the types of graphs that are commonly considered.
   a. Partial equivalence relation
   b. Graph theory
   c. Discrete mathematics
   d. Pooling design

44. For reference, this article details the various tables referenced in the _____ block cipher.

All bits and bytes are arranged in big endian order in this document. That is, bit number 1 is always the most significiant bit.

a. Vampire
b. Battleship
c. Polar coordinate
d. Data Encryption Standard

Chapter 9. Game Theory with an Introduction to Linear Programming

1. A _____ is a structured activity, usually undertaken for enjoyment and sometimes also used as an educational tool. _____s are distinct from work, which is usually carried out for remuneration, and from art, which is more concerned with the expression of ideas. However, the distinction is not clear-cut, and many _____s are also considered to be work (such as professional players of spectator sports/_____s) or art (such as jigsaw puzzles or _____s involving an artistic layout such as Mah-jongg solitaire.)
   a. 120-cell
   b. 2-3 heap
   c. 1-center problem
   d. Game

2. In combinatorial game theory, a _____ is a directed graph whose nodes are positions in a game and whose edges are moves. The complete _____ for a game is the _____ starting at the initial position and containing all possible moves from each position. The first two ply of the _____ for tic-tac-toe.

   The diagram shows the first two levels, or ply, in the _____ for tic-tac-toe.
   a. Surreal number
   b. 120-cell
   c. Game tree
   d. 1-center problem

3. In set theory, a _____ is a partially ordered set such that for each t ∈ T, the set {s ∈ T : s < t} is well-ordered by the relation <. For each t ∈ T, the order type of {s ∈ T : s < t} is called the height of t. The height of T itself is the least ordinal greater than the height of each element of T.
   a. Set-theoretic topology
   b. Definable numbers
   c. Transitive reduction
   d. Tree

4. A _____ is a 2D geometric symbolic representation of information according to some visualization technique. Sometimes, the technique uses a 3D visualization which is then projected onto the 2D surface. The word graph is sometimes used as a synonym for _____.
   a. 120-cell
   b. 1-center problem
   c. 2-3 heap
   d. Diagram

Chapter 9. Game Theory with an Introduction to Linear Programming

5. In game theory, a player's _____ in a game is a complete plan of action for whatever situation might arise; this fully determines the player's behaviour. A player's _____ will determine the action the player will take at any stage of the game, for every possible history of play up to that stage.

A _____ profile is a set of strategies for each player which fully specifies all actions in a game.

  a. Sir Philip Sidney game
  b. Correlated equilibrium
  c. Matching pennies
  d. Strategy

6. _____ is an abbreviation for Cryptographic Hardware and Embedded Systems, a workshop for cryptography research, focusing on hardware-related topics. _____ is a workshop sponsored by the International Association for Cryptologic Research. _____ was first held in Worcester, Massachusetts in 1999 at Worcester Polytechnic Institute.
  a. HC-256
  b. NLFSR
  c. Zimmermann-Sassaman key-signing protocol
  d. Ches

7. _____ is a two-player mathematical game of strategy in which players take turns removing objects from distinct heaps. On each turn, a player must remove at least one object, and may remove any number of objects provided they all come from the same heap.

Variants of _____ have been played since ancient times.

  a. Subtract-a-square
  b. Nim
  c. 1-center problem
  d. Ghost Leg

8. In geometry, a _____ is a special kind of point, usually a corner of a polygon, polyhedron, or higher dimensional polytope. In the geometry of curves a _____ is a point of where the first derivative of curvature is zero. In graph theory, a _____ is the fundamental unit out of which graphs are formed
  a. Vertex
  b. Duality
  c. Dini
  d. Crib

Chapter 9. Game Theory with an Introduction to Linear Programming

9. In mathematics, a _____ is a rectangular table of elements, which may be numbers or, more generally, any abstract quantities that can be added and multiplied. Matrices are used to describe linear equations, keep track of the coefficients of linear transformations and to record data that depend on multiple parameters. Matrices are described by the field of _____ theory.

   a. Matrix
   b. Double counting
   c. Compression
   d. Coherent

10. In mathematics, the point $\tilde{\mathbf{x}} \in \mathbb{R}^n$ is an _____ for the differential equation

$$\frac{d\mathbf{x}}{dt} = \mathbf{f}(t, \mathbf{x})$$

if $\mathbf{f}(t, \tilde{\mathbf{x}}) = \mathbf{0}$ for all t.

Similarly, the point $\tilde{\mathbf{x}} \in \mathbb{R}^n$ is an _____ for the difference equation

$$\mathbf{x}_{k+1} = \mathbf{f}(k, \mathbf{x}_k)$$

if $\mathbf{f}(k, \tilde{\mathbf{x}}) = \tilde{\mathbf{x}}$ for $k = 0, 1, 2, \ldots$.

Equilibria can be classified by looking at the signs of the eigenvalues of the linearization of the equations about the equilibria.

   a. Algorithm design
   b. Unitary transformation
   c. Uniform algebra
   d. Equilibrium point

11. In model theory, a complete theory is called _____ if it does not have too many types. One goal of classification theory is to divide all complete theories into those whose models can be classified and those whose models are too complicated to classify, and to classify all models in the cases where this can be done. Roughly speaking, if a theory is not _____ then its models are too complicated and numerous to classify, while if a theory is _____ there might be some hope of classifying its models, especially if the theory is superstable or totally transcendental.

a. Transfer principle
b. Stable
c. Non-standard calculus
d. Spectrum of a theory

12. The game of _____ is an influential model of conflict for two players in game theory. The principle of the game is that while each player prefers not to yield to the other, the outcome where neither player yields is the worst possible one for both players. The name '_____' has its origins in a game in which two drivers drive towards each other on a collision course: one must swerve, or both may die in the crash, but if one driver swerves and the other does not, the one who swerved will be called a '_____,' meaning a coward; this terminology is most prevalent in the political science and economics.
    a. Bounded rationality
    b. Graph continuous
    c. Complete mixing
    d. Chicken

13. _____, is a popular two-person hand game.

The game is often used as a selection method in a similar way to coin flipping or drawing straws to randomly select a person for some purpose. However, unlike truly random selections, it can be played with skill if the game extends over many sessions, as a player can often recognize and exploit the non-random behavior of an opponent.

    a. Cube
    b. Monty Hall problem
    c. Prisoner's Dilemma
    d. Rock-Paper-Scissors

14. In mathematics, a _____ is a point in the domain of a function of two variables which is a stationary point but not a local extremum. At such a point, in general, the surface resembles a saddle that curves up in one direction, and curves down in a different direction. In terms of contour lines, a _____ can be recognized, in general, by a contour that appears to intersect itself.
    a. 1-center problem
    b. Gauss-Codazzi equations
    c. Gauss map
    d. Saddle point

15. In probability theory and statistics, the _____ of a random variable is the integral of the random variable with respect to its probability measure. For discrete random variables this is equivalent to the probability-weighted sum of the possible values, and for continuous random variables with a density function it is the probability density -weighted integral of the possible values.

The _____ may be intuitively understood by the law of large numbers: The _____, when it exists, is almost surely the limit of the sample mean as sample size grows to infinity.

  a. Expected value
  b. Illustration
  c. Event
  d. Infinitely divisible distribution

16. In statistical decision theory, where we are faced with the problem of estimating a deterministic parameter $\theta \in \Theta$ from observations $x \in \mathcal{X}$. An estimator δ^M is called _____ if it's maximal risk is minimal among all estimators of θ. In a sense this means that δ^M is an estimator which performs best in the worst possible case allowed in the problem.
  a. Regret
  b. Gittins index
  c. Championship mobilization
  d. Minimax

17. _____ was a Hungarian American mathematician who made major contributions to a vast range of fields, including set theory, functional analysis, quantum mechanics, ergodic theory, continuous geometry, economics and game theory, computer science, numerical analysis, hydrodynamics, and statistics, as well as many other mathematical fields. He is generally regarded as one of the foremost mathematicians of the 20th century. The mathematician Jean Dieudonné called von Neumann 'the last of the great mathematicians.' Most notably, von Neumann was a pioneer of the application of operator theory to quantum mechanics, a principal member of the Manhattan Project and the Institute for Advanced Study in Princeton, and a key figure in the development of game theory and the concepts of cellular automata and the universal constructor.
  a. Hemachandra SurÄ«
  b. Stuart Milner-Barry
  c. John von Neumann
  d. Frederick William Winterbotham

18. In mathematics, a _____ is a statement that can be proved on the basis of explicitly stated or previously agreed assumptions.

a. Disjunction introduction
b. Theorem
c. Boolean function
d. Logical value

19. In mathematics, _____ is a technique for optimization of a linear objective function, subject to linear equality and linear inequality constraints. Informally, _____ determines the way to achieve the best outcome in a given mathematical model given some list of requirements represented as linear equations.

More formally, given a polytope, and a real-valued affine function

$$f(x_1, x_2, \ldots, x_n) = c_1 x_1 + c_2 x_2 + \cdots + c_n x_n + d$$

defined on this polytope, a _____ method will find a point in the polytope where this function has the smallest value.

a. Descent direction
b. Linear programming relaxation
c. Linear programming
d. Lin-Kernighan

20. In geometry, a _____ or n-_____ is an n-dimensional analogue of a triangle. Specifically, a _____ is the convex hull of a set of affinely independent points in some Euclidean space of dimension n or higher.

For example, a 0-_____ is a point, a 1-_____ is a line segment, a 2-_____ is a triangle, a 3-_____ is a tetrahedron, and a 4-_____ is a pentachoron.

a. Hypercell
b. Polytetrahedron
c. Simplex
d. Demihypercubes

21. In mathematical optimization theory, the simplex algorithm, created by the American mathematician George Dantzig in 1947, is a popular algorithm for numerical solution of the linear programming problem. The journal Computing in Science and Engineering listed it as one of the top 10 algorithms of the century.

An unrelated, but similarly named method is the Nelder-Mead method or downhill _____ due to Nelder ' Mead and is a numerical method for optimising many-dimensional unconstrained problems, belonging to the more general class of search algorithms.

a. Differential evolution
b. Fibonacci search
c. Hill climbing
d. Simplex method

22. In game theory, _____s are a class of games with multiple pure strategy Nash equilibria in which players choose the same or corresponding strategies. _____s are a formalization of the idea of a coordination problem, which is widespread in the social sciences, including economics, meaning situations in which all parties can realize mutual gains, but only by making mutually consistent decisions. A common application is the choice of technological standards.

a. Cook reduction
b. Coordinate vector
c. Coordination game
d. Continuous wavelet

23. In game theory, a _____ is a solution that people will tend to use in the absence of communication, because it seems natural, special or relevant to them. The concept was introduced by the Nobel Prize winning American economist Thomas Schelling in his book The Strategy of Conflict. In this book, Schelling describes 'focal point[s] for each person's expectation of what the other expects him to expect to be expected to do.' This type of focal point later was named after Schelling.

a. Subgame perfect equilibrium
b. Chainstore paradox
c. Complete information
d. Schelling point

24. _____ is an important concept in economics with broad applications in game theory, engineering and the social sciences. The term is named after Vilfredo Pareto, an Italian economist who used the concept in his studies of economic efficiency and income distribution.

Given a set of alternative allocations of, say, goods or income for a set of individuals, a change from one allocation to another that can make at least one individual better off without making any other individual worse off is called a Pareto improvement.

a. Pursuit-evasion
b. Multiunit auction
c. Quasi-perfect equilibrium
d. Pareto efficiency

ANSWER KEY

Chapter 1
1. b 2. c 3. a 4. d 5. d 6. d 7. a 8. d 9. d 10. b
11. a 12. a 13. c

Chapter 2
1. d 2. c 3. d 4. a 5. d 6. d 7. d 8. d 9. b 10. d

Chapter 3
1. d 2. d 3. d 4. c 5. a 6. d 7. d 8. c 9. d 10. b
11. d 12. d 13. b 14. d 15. c 16. b

Chapter 4
1. d 2. d 3. c 4. a 5. a 6. b 7. a 8. d 9. c 10. c
11. d 12. d 13. a 14. d 15. c 16. a 17. a 18. d 19. d 20. d
21. a 22. d 23. d

Chapter 5
1. d 2. d 3. b 4. c 5. d 6. d 7. d 8. c 9. b 10. c
11. c 12. d 13. c 14. c 15. d 16. c 17. b 18. b 19. c 20. a
21. d 22. c 23. b 24. d 25. d 26. a 27. d 28. b 29. b 30. d
31. d 32. a 33. b 34. a 35. d 36. a 37. b

Chapter 6
1. d 2. c 3. a 4. d 5. d 6. a 7. b 8. a 9. d 10. c
11. d 12. b 13. d 14. b 15. d 16. d 17. d 18. d 19. a 20. d
21. a

Chapter 7
1. b 2. c 3. b 4. b 5. a 6. a 7. d 8. c 9. b 10. d
11. c 12. a 13. d 14. d 15. d 16. d 17. b 18. a 19. c

Chapter 8
1. c 2. d 3. d 4. a 5. c 6. d 7. b 8. d 9. d 10. a
11. d 12. d 13. a 14. c 15. c 16. c 17. b 18. d 19. c 20. d
21. d 22. d 23. a 24. a 25. d 26. b 27. a 28. d 29. d 30. d
31. b 32. c 33. a 34. d 35. a 36. d 37. d 38. d 39. d 40. d
41. b 42. d 43. b 44. d

Chapter 9
1. d 2. c 3. d 4. d 5. d 6. d 7. b 8. a 9. a 10. d
11. b 12. d 13. d 14. d 15. a 16. d 17. c 18. b 19. c 20. c
21. d 22. c 23. d 24. d